R Programming

Simply In Depth

By Ajit Singh

R Programming : Simply In Depth

Contents

Preface

This book will teach you how to program in R. You'll go from loading data to writing your own functions (which will outperform the functions of other R users).This is an understandable approach to learning R. Visualizing and modeling data are complicated skills that require a programmer's full attention. It takes expertise, judgement, and focus to extract reliable insights from a data set.

Introduction

The R Project for Statistical Computing (http://www.r-project.org/)

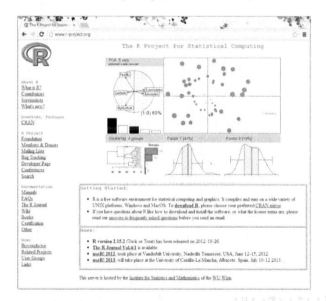

What is R?

The R Project for Statistical Computing (http://www.r-project.org/).

- R is a language and environment for statistical computing and graphics.
- It is similar to the S language (Bell Laboratories, 1970). The R project was initiated by Robert Gentleman and Ross Ihaka (University of Auckland, New Zealand, in the early 1990s) and has been developed with contributions from all over the world since mid-1997.
- R provides a wide variety of statistical and graphical techniques, and is highly extensible (active community of developers).
- R is available as Free Software.

Installation

- The R system consists on two major parts:
  - The base system (what you need to install R for the first time).
  - The collection of contributed packages.

- Sources, binaries and documentation for R can be obtained via CRAN (Comprehensive R Archive Network).

- Choose a location in http://cran.r-project.org/mirrors.html.

- For most users (Windows, MacOS X and some Linux distributions) is sufficient to download and install precompiled binaries for base distribution (following the instructions by the installer).

- Run the setup program (.exe in Windows, .app in Mac).

- By default, R is installed into %ProgramFiles%R.

 R Core Team (2012). More bibliography

R Installation and Administration. R Foundation for Statistical Computing. Vienna, Austria.
ISBN 3-900051-09-7

http://cran.r-project.org/doc/manuals/R-admin.html

Documentation in R

Different forms of documentation for the R system:

- Electronic manuals.
  http://cran.r-project.org/manuals.html
- A wide collection of books and other publications related to R.
  http://www.r-project.org/doc/bib/R-publications.html
  http://www.r-project.org/other-docs.html
- R FAQ.
  http://cran.r-project.org/doc/FAQ/R-FAQ.html
- Online help (with the base distribution and packages).

My first session in R

To run R, click on the R icon (or go to Programs ı R).

Inside the R GUI window, there is a menu bar, a toolbar, and the R console.

Figure: R's graphical user interface for Windows

The R console

- The R console is where you type commands and R system responds.
- This window displays basic information about R and a command prompt >.
- The prompt > indicates that R is waiting for you to type commands.
- Sometimes the symbol + appears at the left-hand side of the screen instead of >. This means that the last command you typed is incomplete.

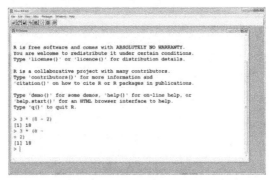

Figure: R as a calculator. The [1] indicates that this is the first (and in this case only) result from the command

The R console

At its most basic level, R can be viewed as a calculator. The elementary arithmetic operators are +, -, *, / and ^ for raising to a power.

```
> 7 * (3 + 2)/2
[1] 17.5
> 2^3
[1] 8
```

Most of the work in R is done through functions. For example, if we want to compute $\sqrt{9}$ in R we type:

```
> sqrt(9)
[1] 3
```

This tells R to call the function named sqrt. The parentheses surround the argument list.

The natural logarithm can be computed with the function log.

```
> log(5)
[1] 1.609
```

Numeric functions

R function	Description
sqrt (x)	square root of x
exp (x)	exponential function e^x
log (x)	natural logarithm of x
log10 (x)	common logarithm of x
abs (x)	absolute value of x
sin (x)	sine of x
cos (x)	cosine of x
tan (x)	tangent of x

Online help

- Once R is installed, there is a comprehensive built-in help system.
- For general help type:

```
> help.start()
```

- For help about a function:

```
> help(log) # Equivalent to ?log
```

- You can also list all functions containing a given string.

```
> apropos("log")
```

- To show an example of a function, type:

```
> example(log)
```

First objects

- R lets you assign values to variables and refer to them by name.
- In R, we use the symbol <- for assigning values to variables. We can see the results of the assignment by typing the name of our new object.

```
> x <- 3
> x

[1] 3
```

- The equals sign = can also be used as assignment operator in most circumstances.

```
> y = 5
> y

[1] 5
```

- R is case sensitive so X is not the same as x.

```
> X

Error: object 'X' not found
```

- Variable names should not begin with numbers or symbols and should not contain blank spaces.

First objects

Character strings in R are made with matching quotes:

```
> myname <- "Bea"
> myname

[1] "Bea"
```

TRUE and FALSE are reserved words denoting logical constants in the R language.

```
> mylog <- TRUE
> mylog

[1] TRUE
```

Special values used in R

- The NA values represent missing values (not available).
- Positive and negative infinity are represented with Inf and -Inf, repectively:

```
> 1/0
[1] Inf
> -5/0
[1] -Inf
```

- In R, NaN stands for "Not a Number".

```
> sqrt(-4)
Warning: NaNs produced
[1] NaN
```

Workspace

- We have created several simple R objects. These objects are stored in the current R workspace. To see what objects are currently defined type:

```
> objects()
```

- This is equivalent to:

```
> ls()
```

- An object can be removed using the function remove or, equivalently, rm.

```
> rm(x)
```

- To clear the workspace use:

```
> rm(list = ls())
```

Workspace

To quit (exit) R use:[1]

```
> q ()
```

We have the option of saving the workspace in a file called a workspace image. If we quit the R session without saving the workspace, then the objects we have created will disappear. If we choose to save the workspace, then the workspace image will be saved in the current working directory as a file called .RData and restored at our next R session. (The .RData file is loaded by default when R is started).

It is also possible to save the workspace image without quitting.

```
> save. image ()
```

We could save the current session to a file called myWspace.RData by typing:[2]

```
> save. image ("myWspace.RData")
```

The workspace image will be saved in the current working directory.

---

[1] You can also use the menu option File ¦ Exit
[2] You can also use the menu option File ¦ Save Workspace...

Workspace

The working directory is the default place where R looks for files that are read from disk, or written to disk. The current working directory is obtained with:

```
> getwd()
```

We can also set the working directory using the function setwd.[3]

```
> setwd("C:/Users/beatriz/Documents/Rwork")
> getwd()

[1] "C:/Users/beatriz/Documents/Rwork"
```

In this example the command setwd only works if the directory RWork already exists.

We can now save the workspace in the current directory and quit:

```
> save.image("myWspace2.RData")
> q(save = "no")
```

In the last line we avoid R asking again whether it should save the workspace.

---

[3] You can also use the menu option File ı   Change dir...

Workspace

We can begin an R session with the workspace image we saved earlier called myWspace2.RData, by clicking on the icon for myWspace2.RData.

Figure: **Saved workspace image** (.RData)

Alternatively, we can use the function load.[4]

```
> load("myWspace2.RData")
```

In this example the command load only works if myWspace2.RData is in the current working directory. Otherwise, you should specify the complete path to the file or change the working directory before loading the file.

---

[4] You can also use the menu option File ⁞ Load Workspace...

Workspace

- It is a good idea to save the workspace only if your calculations take a long time to complete.
- Rather than saving the workspace, it is more convenient to keep a record of the commands we entered, so that we can reproduce the workspace at a later date.

Scripts

The simplest way to keep a record of the commands is to enter commands using the default editor that comes with R.

An R script is simply a text file containing the same commands that you would enter on the command line of R.

Use the menu option File ɪ   New Script to create a new R script.

Figure: R's script editor

Scripts

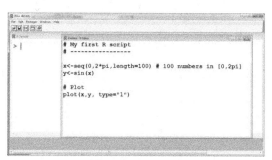

Figure: My first R script

- The symbol # indicates a comment. All characters following # until the end of the line are ignored.

- The R code can be executed by copying and pasting code into the R console or by selecting code and pressing Ctrl + R (in Windows).[5]

- Save the script file as FirstScript.R in the directory RWork with the menu option File ⌐ Save as...

---

[5] You can also use the menu options Edit ⌐ Run line or selection or Edit ⌐ Run all

Scripts

The source function runs a script in the current session. If the filename does not include a path, the file is taken from the current working directory.

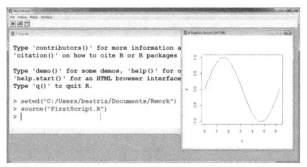

Figure: My first R script

Packages

- All R functions and datasets are stored in packages.
- Only when a package is loaded are its contents available.
- Some packages are installed with R and automatically loaded at the start of an R session. The standard packages contain the basic functions that allow R to work, and the datasets and standard statistical and graphical functions. These include:
  - The base package, where functions such as sqrt are defined.
  - The graphics package, which allows plots to be generated.
  - The stats package, which provides a broad range of statistical functionality.
- The function library without any arguments returns a list of all currently installed packages.

```
> library()
```

Packages

- There are thousands of contributed packages for R. Some of them implement specialized statistical methods, others give access to data, and others are designed to complement textbooks. (5)
- Contributed packages can be downloaded and installed with the install.packages function.[6] For example, to download and install the package rugarch[7], type:

```
> install.packages("rugarch")
```

- In order to use a package, it needs to be loaded with the function library.[8]

```
> library(rugarch)
```

- For help about a package:

```
> help(package = rugarch)
```

[6] You can also use the menu option Packages → Install packages...

[7] The rugarch package provides methods for modeling univariate GARCH processes, including fitting, filtering, forecasting, simulation as well as diagnostic tools including plots and various tests

[8] You can also use the menu option Packages → Load package...

Packages

- In addition to the help files, R packages allow the inclusion of vignettes. A vignette is a PDF document that provides a description of package functionality and contains executable examples.

- The function `vignette` without any arguments returns a list of the vignettes for the currently installed packages.

```
> vignette()
```

- The package rugarch includes the vignette Introduction_to_the_rugarch_package. You can access the PDF version of the vignette as follows:

```
> vignette("Introduction_to_the_rugarch_package")
```

Packages

- R packages also allow the inclusion of data sets.

- The function data without any arguments returns a list of the data sets for the currently installed packages.

```
> data()
```

- The package rugarch includes the data set sp500ret. To obtain information about the data set, type:

```
> help(sp500ret)
```

- You can access the data set as follows:

```
> data(sp500ret)
> sp500ret
```

External editors

- There are also external editors that have modes for highlighting R syntax and executing code directly from the editor.
  - RStudio
    http://www.rstudio.com/
  - Notepad++ (with NppToR)
    http://notepad-plus-plus.org/
  - Tinn-R
    http://www.sciviews.org/Tinn-R/
  - Eclipse (with StatET)
    http://www.eclipse.org/
  - ...

RStudio

- RStudio is a free and open source integrated development environment for R.
- It combines all resources required for programming in R in a single window.
- The standard layout consists of the source editor, the workspace and history pane, the files, help and graphics browser, and the R-console.

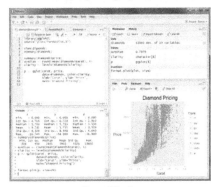

Figure: **RStudio**

Tools and features

- Multi-platform.
- Syntax highlighting, code completion.
- Execute R code directly from the editor.
- Workspace browser and data viewer.
- Integrated R help and documentation.
- It supports Sweave, knitr, R markdown and LaTeX. [7]

Table of contents. Working with data

Importing data

- We have seen how to load data sets included in packages with the function data.
- However, we use to work with our own data sets.
- We will describe different ways to import data into the R system.
- R can import data from text files, other statistics software, spreadsheets or a even from a web address (URL).

 R Core Team (2012). More bibliography
R Data Import/Export. R Foundation for Statistical Computing. Vienna, Austria. ISBN 3-900051-10-0
http://cran.r-project.org/doc/manuals/R-data.html

 J. Adler (2010).
R in a Nutshell (Chapter 12).
O'Reilly Media. ISBN 9781449383046. Google books

Importing data from text files

- The simplest way to store data is in a plain text file (with the columns containing variables and the rows containing observations).

- The function read.table is the most convenient way to read in a rectangular grid of data from a text file.

- We first check the help file for the function read.table:

```
> help(read.table)
```

- The first argument of the function read.table is:
    - file: the name of the file which the data are to be read from.

- There are other arguments to control the format of the input file, such as:
    - header: a logical value (TRUE or FALSE) indicating whether the file contains the names of the variables as its first line (by default header = FALSE).
    - sep: the field separator character (by default sep = " ").
    - dec: the character used in the file for decimal points (by default dec = ".").

- R functions can have many arguments. Some of them are defined to take default values so that users do not need to provide values for every argument. [48]

Importing data from text files

- We will import data from a very simple text file. Open the file data1.txt with a text editor (Notepad) to see how the data are arranged. Save the file in the directory RWork.

- The file contains five observations for 3 variables (x, y, z). The names of the variables are in the first line (header = TRUE). The columns are separated by white spaces (sep = " "). The character used in the file for decimal points is a dot (dec = ".").

- We write the commands in a new script Importing.R:

```
# Script Importing.R

# Importing data from data1.txt (complete path)
data1 <- read.table("C:/Users/beatriz/Documents/Rwork/data1.txt",
    header = TRUE, sep = " ", dec = ".")
```

Importing data from text files

- Run the code and check that the object data1 has been created.

```
> print(data1) # prints the object data1
    x    y    z
1 1.2  2.5  3.6
2 4.5  5.6  6.4
3 6.7  4.5  9.6
4 5.6   NA  1.2
5 4.8  5.6  7.8
> class(data1)
[1] "data.frame"
> dim(data1)
[1] 5 3
```

- The function read.table returns an object of class data.frame. A data frame is used for storing data tables. It combines variables of equal length. Each row in the data frame contains observations on the same sampling unit. In a data frame we can combine numerical variables, character strings, and factors (categorical variables). Later, we will describe how to work with data frames.

Importing data from text files

Recall that you can change the working directory to the folder where you keep your scripts and data files.

```
# Script Importing.R

# Importing data from data1.txt (complete path)
data1 <- read.table("C:/Users/beatriz/Documents/Rwork/data1.txt",
    header = TRUE, sep = " ", dec = ".")

# Working directory
setwd("C:/Users/beatriz/Documents/Rwork")

# Importing data from data1.txt
data1 <- read.table("data1.txt", header = TRUE, sep = " ", dec = ".")
```

Importing data from text files

Check the default values of the arguments of the function read.table.

```
# Script Importing.R

# Importing data from data1.txt (complete path)
data1 <- read.table("C:/Users/beatriz/Documents/Rwork/data1.txt",
    header = TRUE, sep = " ", dec = ".")

# Working directory
setwd("C:/Users/beatriz/Documents/Rwork")

# Importing data from data1.txt
data1 <- read.table("C:/Users/beatriz/Documents/Rwork/data1.txt",
    header = TRUE, sep = " ", dec = ".")
```

Importing data from text files

- The function read.table is very flexible and allows you to load files with many different formats.

- R includes a set of functions that call read.table with different default options for some arguments. [40]

R function	header	sep	dec
read.table	FALSE	" "	"."
read.csv	TRUE	","	"."
read.csv2	TRUE	";"	","
read.delim	TRUE	"\t"	"."
read.delim2	TRUE	"\t"	","

- For example, we import into R the data in the file data2.txt:

```
# Script Importing.R (... continuation)

# Importing data from data2.txt
data2 <- read.table("data2.txt", header = TRUE, sep = ",")

# The previous call is equivalent to:
data2 <- read.csv("data2.txt")
```

Importing data from a URL

- The function read.table (or any of its variations) can also read directly from a URL, by giving the URL as the file argument.

- For example, the Brazilian Institute of Geography and Statistics[9] provides historical time series in a downloadable form on the website http://seriesestatisticas.ibge.gov.br

- You can fetch a .xls file from a single URL. For example, to fetch the INCP[10] series for metropolitan regions between January, 2012, and February, 2013 you could use the following code:

```
# Script Importing.R (... continuation)

# Importing data from URL (copy in the same line)
data3 <- read.delim2("http://seriesestatisticas.ibge.gov.br/
                exportador.aspx?arquivo=PC51_RM_PERC.csv&
                categorias=%22Indice%20geral%22&
                localidade=Todas")
```

---

[9] http://www.ibge.gov.br/

[10] Índice Nacional de Preços ao Consumidor

Importing data from Excel

The easiest way to read data from a spreadsheet program into R is to export it to a text file and use the read.table function (or any of its variations). For example, for Microsoft Excel spreadsheets and Apache OpenOffice Calc spreadsheets, you can export them as either comma-separated values files or tab-separated values files and use read.csv or read.delim in R. [410]

Importing data from Excel

It is also possible to read data files from Excel directly into R. Windows users (of 32-bit R) can use the odbcConnectExcel function in package RODBC.[11] The function odbcConnectExcel can select rows and columns from any of the sheets in an Excel spreadsheet file.

```
# Importing data from Excel with RODBC (Windows 32-bit R)
library(RODBC)
# Open a connection to the file
conex <- odbcConnectExcel("serie_INCP.xls")
# List of worksheet tab names
sqlTables(conex)
# Read the table INCP into a data frame
data4 <- sqlFetch(conex, "INCP")
# Close the connection
close(conex)
```

---

[11] The package RODBC provides the tools to access databases through an ODBC interface.

Importing data from statistical systems

The package foreign provides import facilities for files produced by S-PLUS, SAS, SPSS, Stata, and other statistical systems.

```
library(foreign)
help(package = foreign)
```

Importing data from databases

- R communicates with database management systems.
- In order to connect to a database from R, you will need to install some optional packages.
- There are several packages available in R:
  - The RODBC package: provides the tools to access databases through an ODBC interface. (You may need to install the ODBC drivers for your platform).
  - The DBI package: it is a set of packages (RMySQL, ROracle, ...) for accessing databases from R.

 R Core Team (2012).
R Data Import/Export. R Foundation for Statistical Computing. Vienna, Austria. ISBN 3-900051-10-0 (Chapter 4)
http://cran.r-project.org/doc/manuals/R-data.html

(More bibliography)

Exporting data

- R can also export R data objects as text file with the function `write.table`
- Let us export the object data1 as a text file.

```
# Script Importing.R (... continuation)

# Exporting data1 to data1export.txt
write.table(data1, file = "data1export.txt", sep = ";",
            row.names = FALSE, col.names = FALSE)
```

- Check that the file data1export.txt has been saved in the working directory. We chose the semicolon as delimiter character. The row and column names of data1 were not included in the file.

- You can also export the object as a comma-separated values files with the functions `write.csv` and `write.csv2`.

```
# Exporting data1 to data1export.csv
write.csv2(data1, file="data1export.csv")
```

- The function `write.foreign` in package `foreign` exports data frames to other statistical packages.

Objects and classes

- When we enter data in R (either manually or by importing from a text file) we create an object.

- R has a wide variety of data objects such as vectors (numerical, character, logical), factors, matrices and arrays, lists, data frames, ...

- All objects in R have a class. The class of an object determines the methods that will be used to handle it. For example, an object of class data.frame will be printed in a certain way (printing a data frame is different from printing a vector of numbers). What the functions print does depends on the class of its argument.

- An object in R can have many properties associated with it (attributes). For example, the class of an object is implemented as an attribute.

- The type of an object defines how it is stored in R.

Objects and classes. Examples

- Object of class `matrix`.

```
> data(USPersonalExpenditure) # United States personal expenditures
> class(USPersonalExpenditure)

[1] "matrix"
```

- Time series object of class `ts`.

```
> data(AirPassengers) # Box & Jenkins airline data
> class(AirPassengers)

[1] "ts"
```

- Time series object of class `timeSeries`.

```
> library(timeSeries)
> data(MSFT) # Daily Microsoft OHLC prices and volume
> class(MSFT)

[1] "timeSeries"
attr(,"package")
[1] "timeSeries"
```

Vectors

- A vector is an object that consists of a number of elements of the same type: integers, floating-point numbers, complex numbers, text, or logical values.

- The simplest way to store a number of elements of the same type in R is through the c command, that concatenates the values into a single object. For example:[12]

```
> v <- c(4, 5, 23.8, 67) # a vector of four numbers
> w <- c(14, 35)
> x <- c(v, w)
> x

[1] 4.0 5.0 23.8 67.0 14.0 35.0

> class(x)

[1] "numeric"

> typeof(x)

[1] "double"
```

---

[12] In this example we simply write commands in the R console. However, it is recommended that you write your commands in a script and then run the commands from the script.

Vectors

We can also use the c command to create a string of characters. For example:

```
> z <- c("yes", "no")
> z
[1] "yes" "no"
> class(z)
[1] "character"
```

Vectors

We can use the c command to create a logical vector:

```
> v <- c(FALSE, FALSE, TRUE, FALSE)
> v
[1] FALSE FALSE TRUE FALSE
> class(v)
[1] "logical"
```

Vectors

All elements of a vector have the same type. If we concatenate elements of different types, the vector will have the least "restrictive" type. For instance, if we concatenate numbers and characters, the resulting vector has type character.

```
> v <- c(3, 5, "yes")
> v
[1] "3"   "5"   "yes"
> class(v)
[1] "character"
```

If we concatenate numbers and logicals, the resulting vector has type numeric.

```
> v <- c(3, 5, TRUE, FALSE)
> v
[1] 3 5 1 0
> class(v)
[1] "numeric"
```

Vectors

- Apart from the command c, there are other useful functions to create vectors in various situations.
- The function seq is used to generate equidistant series of numbers.
- Open the help file of the function seq and check that the arguments of the function are (in order): from, to, by, length.out and along.with.
- To generate a sequence of values between two points with a given length, use:

```
> s1 <- seq(1, 8, length = 5) # 5 equidistant numbers from 1 to 8
> s1

[1] 1.00 2.75 4.50 6.25 8.00
```

- To generate a sequence of values between two points with a given step size, use:

```
> s2 <- seq(1, 10, by = 2) # from 1 to 10 with step size 2
> s2

[1] 1 3 5 7 9
```

Vectors

The case with step size equal to 1 (or -1) can also be written using ":".

```
> seq(1, 10, by = 1)
 [1] 1 2 3 4 5 6 7 8 9 10
> 1:10
 [1] 1 2 3 4 5 6 7 8 9 10
> 7:3
[1] 7 6 5 4 3
```

Vectors

The function rep is used to generate repeated values.

```
> rep(2, 3) # Repeat the number 2 three times
[1] 2 2 2
> rep(TRUE, 5)
[1] TRUE TRUE TRUE TRUE TRUE
>rep(1:4, 3) # Repeat the vector [1, 2, 3, 4] three times
 [1] 1 2 3 4 1 2 3 4 1 2 3 4
>rep(1:4, each = 3) # Each element of [1, 2, 3, 4] is repeated 3 times
 [1] 1 1 1 2 2 2 3 3 3 4 4 4
```

Vector arithmetics

Vectors can be used in arithmetic expressions.   The operations are performed element by element.

```
> v1 <- c(3, 6, 2)
> v2 <- c(1, 5, 3)
> v1 + v2

[1] 4 11 5
>v1 * v2

[1] 3 30 6
```

Vectors in the same expression need not all be of the same length. Shorter vectors are recycled until they match the length of the longest vector. In particular,

```
> v1 + 7

[1] 10 13 9
```

All of the common arithmetic functions are also available: log, exp, sqrt,...

```
> sqrt(v1)

[1] 1.732 2.449 1.414
```

Vector operators and functions

R offers functions designed to work on a vector x.

R function	Description
sum(x)	sum of all the values of x
prod(x)	product of all the values of x
max(x)	maximum value of x
min(x)	minimum value of x
length(x)	length of x
sort(x)	sort the vector x into ascending order
mean(x)	arithmetic mean of x

Matrices

- A matrix is a collection of data elements arranged in a two-dimensional grid (rows and columns).

- As with vectors, all the elements of a matrix must be of the same data type.

- A matrix can be generated in several ways. The function matrix creates a matrix from a given set of values. For example, we create a matrix with the numbers from 10 to 15 with 2 rows and 3 columns.

```
> a <- matrix(10:15, nrow = 2, ncol = 3)
> a

     [,1] [,2] [,3]
[1,]   10   12   14
[2,]   11   13   15

> class(a)

[1] "matrix"

> typeof(a)

[1] "integer"
```

Matrices

- By default, the function matrix fills in the matrix column by column. Set the argument byrow = TRUE to fill in the matrix row by row.

```
> b <- matrix(10:15, nrow = 2, ncol = 3, byrow = TRUE)
> b

     [,1] [,2] [,3]
[1,]   10   11   12
[2,]   13   14   15

> dim(b) # Dimension

[1] 2 3
```

Matrices

- Other useful functions to define matrices are cbind and rbind.
- The function cbind creates a matrix by binding two or more vectors as column vectors and the function rbind creates a matrix by binding two or more vectors as row vectors.

```
> x <- 1:3
> y <- 7:9
> m1 <- cbind(x, y)
> m1

     x y
[1,] 1 7
[2,] 2 8
[3,] 3 9

> m2 <- rbind(x, y)
> m2

  [,1] [,2] [,3]
x    1    2    3
y    7    8    9
```

Matrix arithmetics

Matrices may be used in arithmetic expressions and the result is a matrix formed by element-by-element operations.

```
> a + b

     [, 1] [, 2] [, 3]
[1,]   20   23   26
[2,]   24   27   30

> a * b # element-by-element product

     [, 1] [, 2] [, 3]
[1,]  100  132  168
[2,]  143  182  225
```

The operator %*% is used for matrix multiplication

```
> m2 %*% m1 # matrix multiplication

    x   y
x  14  50
y  50 194
```

Matrix operators and functions

R offers functions designed to work on a matrix A.

R function	Description
dim(A)	dimension of A
t(A)	transpose the matrix A
solve(A)	inverse of A
eigen(A)	eigenvalues and eigenvectors of A
chol(A)	Choleski decomposition
rowMeans(A)	form row means
rowSums(A)	form row sums
colMeans(A)	form column means
colSums(A)	form column sums

Arrays

An array is an extension of a vector to more than two dimensions.

In R we can generate an array with the array function.

```
> a <- array(data = 1:24, dim = c(3, 4, 2))
> a

, , 1

     [,1] [,2] [,3] [,4]
[1,]    1    4    7   10
[2,]    2    5    8   11
[3,]    3    6    9   12

, , 2

     [,1] [,2] [,3] [,4]
[1,]   13   16   19   22
[2,]   14   17   20   23
[3,]   15   18   21   24
```

Data frames

All elements of a matrix have the same type. Look at what happens when we bind vectors of different types:

```
> name <- c("Mike", "Jane", "Peter")
> age <- c(42, 34, 31)
> dat <- cbind(name, age)
> dat

      name     age
[1,] "Mike"  "42"
[2,] "Jane"  "34"
[3,] "Peter" "31"

> typeof(dat)

[1] "character"
```

Since we bind a numeric vector and a character vector, the result is a matrix where all elements are considered as character. Therefore, the matrix is not the right data structure to store qualitative and quantitative variables together.

Data frames

- Data frames are the primary data structure in R and the natural way to represent tabular data.

- A data frame is an object with rows and columns. It is a more general object than a matrix since different columns may have different types. Each row in the data frame must have the same length.

- We create a data frame with the data.frame function.

```
> dat <- data.frame(name, age)
> dat

   name age
1  Mike  42
2  Jane  34
3 Peter  31

> class(dat)

[1] "data.frame"
```

Data frames

Further properties of an object are usually provided by the function attributes.

```
> attributes(dat)
$names
[1] "name" "age"

$row.names
[1] 1 2 3

$class
[1] "data.frame"
```

Data frames

- We can also get or set specific attributes of an object with the function `attr`.

```
> attr(dat, "description") <- "Names and ages od people"
> attributes(dat)

$names
[1] "name" "age"

$row.names
[1] 1 2 3

$class
[1] "data.frame"

$description
[1] "Names and ages od people"
```

Data frames

The internal structure of an R object can also be displayed with the function `str`.

```
> str(dat)
data.frame : 3 obs. of  2 variables:
$ name: Factor w/ 3 levels "Jane","Mike",..: 2 1 3
$ age : num 42 34 31
- attr(*, "description")= chr "Names and ages od people"
```

Factors

- The best way to represent categorical values in R is as factors, using the function `factor`.

- Suppose we record the blood type of a group of people

```
> blood <- c("AB", "A", "A", "B", "A", "O", "B", "B", "AB")
> fblood <- factor(blood)
> fblood
[1] AB A A B A O B B AB
Levels: O A AB B
```

- A factor is an ordered collection of items. The levels of a factor are the different values that the factor can take.

```
> levels(fblood)
[1] "O" "A" "AB" "B"
```

Factors

- Factors are implemented internally using integers. The levels attribute maps each integer to a factor level.

```
> unclass(fblood) # remove class
[1] 3 2 2 4 2 1 4 4 3
attr(,"levels")
[1] "0" "A" "AB" "B"
```

Lists

A list is a collection of objects (the objects can be of different types).

The function to create lists in R is list.

```
> mylist <- list(s1, dat, fblood) # vector, data.frame and factor
> mylist

[[1]]
[1] 1.00 2.75 4.50 6.25 8.00

[[2]]
   name age
1  Mike  42
2  Jane  34
3 Peter  31

[[3]]
[1] AB A A B A O B B AB
Levels: O A AB B

> class(mylist)

[1] "list"
```

Lists

Elements of lists may also be named.

```
> mylist <- list(sequence = s1, people = dat, bloodtype = fblood)
> mylist

$sequence
[1] 1.00 2.75 4.50 6.25 8.00

$people
   name age
1  Mike  42
2  Jane  34
3 Peter  31

$bloodtype
[1] AB A A B A O B B AB
Levels: O A AB B
```

Lists

Recall that we can display the internal structure of an R object with `str`.

```
> str(mylist)
List of 3
$ sequence : num [1:5] 1 2.75 4.5 6.25 8
$ people   : data.frame : 3 obs. of  2 variables:
 ..$ name: Factor w/ 3 levels "Jane","Mike",..: 2 1 3
 ..$ age : num [1:3] 42 34 31
 ..- attr(*, "description")- chr "Names and ages od people"
$ bloodtype: Factor w/ 4 levels "0","A","AB","B": 3 2 2 4 2 1 4 4 3
```

Coercion functions

- We can convert an object from one class to a different one with "as. " functions (as. numeric, as. character, as. matrix, as. data. frame, ...). For **example:**

```
> x <- c(3, 5)
> class(x)

[1] "numeric"

> y <- as.character(x)
> y

[1] "3" "5"

> class(y)

[1] "character"
```

- These "as. " functions are usually accompanied by the corresponding "is. " functions, that check whether an object is of a given class.

```
> is.numeric(y)

[1] FALSE

> is.character(y)

[1] TRUE
```

Object-oriented programming

- Object oriented programming (OOP) is a style of programming that represents concepts as objects and associated procedures known as methods.
- An object is an instance of a class. A method is a function that performs specific calculations on objects of a specific class.

Object-oriented programming

A generic function determines the class of its argument and selects the appropriate method. For example, summary is a generic function in R. When invoked, the function establishes the class of the argument on which it was called and recruits the appropriate summarizing method for that class of object.

```
> x <- rep(1:4, 3) # Vector [1, 2, 3, 4, 1, 2, 3, 4, 1, 2, 3, 4]
> class(x)

[1] "integer"

> summary(x) # Summary integer class
   Min. 1st Qu.  Median   Mean 3rd Qu.    Max.
   1.00    1.75    2.50   2.50    3.25    4.00

> xf <- factor(x)
> class(xf)

[1] "factor"

>summary(xf) # Summary factor class

1 2 3 4

3 3 3 3
```

OOP models: S3 and S4 objects, classes and methods

The S3 system

- S3 is the basis for most of the modeling software in R. S3 objects, classes and methods have been available in R from the beginning.
- In the S3 system classes are attached to objects as simple attributes. (One can make any object an instance of class, by assigning a class attribute).
- Method dispatch looks for the class of the first argument (single-argument dispatch).

```
> class(AirPassengers) # S3 object
[1] "ts"
> attributes(AirPassengers)
$tsp
[1] 1949 1961   12

$class
[1] "ts"
```

OOP models: S3 and S4 objects, classes and methods

The S4 system

- The S3 classes and methods were limited in flexibility. Around 1992 is introduced the concept of classes and methods as known today by S4 classes software.

- In the S4 system, an S4 class gives a rigorous definition of an object.

- Information in S4 classes is organized into slots. Each slot is named and requires a specified class.

- The S4 system supports multiple dispatch.

```
> class(MSFT) # S4 object

[1] "timeSeries"
attr(,"package")
[1] "timeSeries"

> slotNames(MSFT)

[1] ".Data"         "units"          "positions"
[4] "format"        "FinCenter"      "recordIDs"
[7] "title"         "documentation"
```

Accessing subsets of data

In R, brackets [] indicate a subset of a larger object. For example:

```
> v <- c(4, 5, 23.8, 67) # a vector of four numbers
> v[3] # Third element of v

[1] 23.8

> v[2] # Second element of v

[1] 5

>v[-2] # All of v but the second entry

[1] 4.0 23.8 67.0

>v[c(1, 3)] # First and third elements of v

[1] 4.0 23.8
```

Accessing subsets of data

As with vectors, we refer to elements of matrices using square brackets. The rows are referred to by the first (left-hand) subscript and the columns by the second (right-hand) subscript. For example:

```
> a <- matrix(10:15, nrow = 2, ncol = 3)
> a

     [,1] [,2] [,3]
[1,]   10   12   14
[2,]   11   13   15
>a[2, 3] # Element of a in the second row, third column

[1] 15

>a[2, ] # Second row of a

[1] 11 13 15

>a[, 3] # Third column of a

[1] 14 15
```

Note that the result is a vector, with no dimension information kept.

Accessing subsets of data

If we want to maintain the result as a row or column vector, we use the argument drop = FALSE:

```
>    a[2, , drop = FALSE] # Second row of
     a   [,1] [,2] [,3]
[1,]    11   13   15
> a[, 3, drop = FALSE] # Third column of a
     [,1]
[1,]    14
[2,]    15
```

Accessing subsets of data

A data frame can be considered as a generalized matrix. Therefore, all subscripting methods that work on matrices also work on data frames. For example:

```
> name <- c("Mike", "Jane", "Peter")
> age <- c(42, 34, 31)
> dat <- data.frame(name, age)
> dat

  name age
1 Mike  42
2 Jane  34
3 Peter 31

> dat[2, 2]  # Element of dat in the second row, second column

[1] 34

> dat[, 1] # First column of data frame dat

[1] Mike Jane Peter
Levels: Jane Mike Peter
```

Accessing subsets of data

- We can obtain the variable names of a data frame with the function names.

```
> names(dat)
[1] "name" "age"
```

- Individual variables in a data frame can be accessed using the $ notation.

```
> dat$age # Variable age of data frame dat
[1] 42 34 31
> dat$name # Variable name of data frame dat
[1] Mike Jane Peter
Levels: Jane Mike Peter
```

Accessing subsets of data

- All three of the following lines of code produce the same result:

```
> dat$age
[1] 42 34 31
> dat[, 2]
[1] 42 34 31
>dat[, "age"]
[1] 42 34 31
```

Accessing subsets of data

Individual variables in a list can also be accessed using the $ notation.

```
> mylist

$sequence
[1] 1.00 2.75 4.50 6.25 8.00

$people
    name age
1  Mike  42
2  Jane  34
3 Peter  31

$bloodtype
[1] AB A A B A O B B AB
Levels: O A AB B

> mylist$bloodtype

[1] AB A A B A O B B AB
Levels: O A AB B
```

Accessing subsets of data

- You can access an item in the list with `[[]]`.

```
> mylist$bloodtype[[3]]
[1] A
Levels: 0 A AB B
```

Using logical conditions to select subsets

- Consider the data set MSFT in package timeSeries.

```
> data(MSFT) # daily Microsoft OHLC prices and volume
> head(MSFT) # First part of the data set

GMT
           Open   High   Low Close   Volume
2000-09-27 63.44 63.56 59.81 60.62 53077800
2000-09-28 60.81 61.88 60.62 61.31 26180200
2000-09-29 61.00 61.31 58.62 60.31 37026800
2000-10-02 60.50 60.81 58.25 59.12 29281200
2000-10-03 59.56 59.81 56.50 56.56 42687000
2000-10-04 56.38 56.56 54.50 55.44 68226700
```

- In practice, we often need to extract data that satisfy certain criteria. For instance, we may want to select data on trading days on which the closing price was equal to or greater than 72$.

- We can select subsets using logical conditions.

Using logical conditions to select subsets

Next table shows the logical operators in R.

<	less than
<=	less than or equal to
>	greater than
>=	greater than or equal to
==	equal to
!=	not equal to

Using logical conditions to select subsets

- Consider the following vector:

```
> x <- c(3, 5, 1, 2, 7, 6, 4)
```

- The result of the logical operators is a logical vector.

```
> x < 5 # is x less than 5
[1] TRUE FALSE TRUE TRUE FALSE FALSE  TRUE
> x <= 5 # is x less than or equal to 5
[1] TRUE TRUE TRUE TRUE FALSE FALSE  TRUE
> x > 3 # is x greater than 3
[1] FALSE TRUE FALSE FALSE TRUE TRUE  TRUE
> x >= 3 # is x greater than or equal to 3
[1] TRUE TRUE FALSE FALSE TRUE TRUE  TRUE
> x == 2 # is x equal to 2
[1] FALSE FALSE FALSE TRUE FALSE FALSE FALSE
> x != 2 # is x not equal to 2
[1] TRUE TRUE TRUE FALSE TRUE TRUE  TRUE
```

Using logical conditions to select subsets

- The functions `all` and `any` check whether all or at least some entries of a logical vector are TRUE, respectively.

```
> x
[1] 3 5 1 2 7 6 4
> any(x == 2)
[1] TRUE
> all(x == 2)
[1] FALSE
> all(x < 10)
[1] TRUE
```

- The function `which` gives the TRUE indices of a logical object.

```
> which(x == 2) # Fourth element of x is equal two 2
[1] 4
>which(x < 3) # Third and fourth elements of x are lower than 3
[1] 3 4
```

Using logical conditions to select subsets

The following operators can be used for comparisons (element by element) between logical vectors in R.

&	logical "and"
|	logical "or"
!	logical "not"

The operators && and \|\| are the not vectorized counterparts of & and \|. Moreover, these longer forms are evaluated from left to right (the right-hand operand is only evaluated if necessary).

Using logical conditions to select subsets

```
> x
[1] 3 5 1 2 7 6 4
> (x > 2) & (x <= 6) # is x greater than 2 and less than or equal to 6
[1] TRUE TRUE FALSE FALSE FALSE TRUE TRUE
> (x < 2) | (x > 5) # is x less than 2 or greater than 5
[1] FALSE FALSE TRUE FALSE TRUE TRUE FALSE
> !(x > 3) # not [x greater than 3]
[1] TRUE FALSE TRUE TRUE FALSE FALSE FALSE
```

Using logical conditions to select subsets

Now, consider the following example:

```
> y <- c(5, 3, 7, 2, 9)
```

Suppose that we want to extract the values of the vector y which are greater than 5 (that is, the numbers 7 and 9). To understand the details, we will divide the code the into smaller steps. First, we create a logical vector ind:

```
> ind <- y > 5 # is y greater than 5
> ind
[1] FALSE FALSE TRUE FALSE TRUE
```

Next, we pick out the values of the vector y indexed with the logical vector ind. This means that you pick out the values where the logical vector is TRUE.

```
> y[ind]
[1] 7 9
```

The same result can be obtained in just one line of code:

```
> y[y > 5]
[1] 7 9
```

Using logical conditions to select subsets

Consider the MSFT data set. If we want to select data on trading days on which the closing price was equal to or greater than 72$:

```
>MSFT[MSFT$Close >= 72, ]
```

```
GMT
             Open  High   Low Close    Volume
2001-05-08 71.75 72.10 70.75 72.06 37542000
2001-06-05 70.76 73.08 70.50 72.60 44727100
2001-06-06 72.89 73.48 71.55 72.36 40011400
2001-06-07 72.12 73.73 72.08 73.68 33480000
2001-06-08 73.70 73.75 72.05 73.19 25933500
2001-06-11 72.85 72.85 71.51 72.12 23672800
2001-06-12 71.02 72.41 70.81 72.08 33357300
2001-06-28 71.55 76.15 70.53 72.74 64487800
2001-06-29 72.60 73.41 71.40 73.00 47141900
2001-07-19 71.22 73.00 71.22 72.57 38274700
```

Using logical conditions to select subsets

Consider the MSFT data set. If we want to select data on trading days on which the closing price was equal to or greater than 72$ and the opening price was lower than 71.5$:

```
> MSFT[MSFT$Close >= 72 & MSFT$Open < 71.5, ]
GMT
            Open   High   Low Close   Volume
2001-06-05 70.76 73.08 70.50 72.60 44727100
2001-06-12 71.02 72.41 70.81 72.08 33357300
2001-07-19 71.22 73.00 71.22 72.57 38274700
```

Using logical conditions to select subsets

Consider the MSFT data set. If we want to select the volume on trading days on which the closing price was equal to or greater than 72$ and the opening price was lower than 71.5$:

```
> MSFT[MSFT$Close >= 72 & MSFT$Open < 71.5, "Volume"]
GMT
                Volume
2001-06-05 44727100
2001-06-12 33357300
2001-07-19 38274700
```

Summarizing functions

There are two functions that are helpful for summarizing the contents of R objects:
str and summary. The function str gives information about data types and the
function summary gives a collection of summary statistics.

```
> summary(MSFT)
      Open            High            Low
Min.   :40.8    Min.   :44.0    Min.   :40.3
1st Qu.:56.1    1st Qu.:57.4    1st Qu.:54.9
Median :61.9    Median :63.4    Median :60.7
Mean   :61.6    Mean   :62.9    Mean   :60.5
3rd Qu.:68.3    3rd Qu.:69.8    3rd Qu.:67.5
Max.   :73.7    Max.   :76.2    Max.   :72.1
      Close           Volume
Min.   :41.5    Min.   :1.39e+07
1st Qu.:55.9    1st Qu.:3.17e+07
Median :61.9    Median :4.06e+07
Mean   :61.6    Mean   :4.31e+07    3rd
Qu.:68.5    3rd Qu.:5.09e+07    Max.
:73.7    Max.   :1.28e+08
```

Summary measures

Consider the data set dmbp[13] in the rugarch package.

```
> data(dmbp)
> head(dmbp) # First part of the data set.
          V1 V2
1   0.12533  0
2   0.02887  0
3   0.06346  0
4   0.22672  1
5  -0.21427  0
6   0.20285  0
```

The data set contains the daily percentage nominal returns and a dummy variable that takes the value of 1 on Mondays and other days following no trading in the Deutschemark or British pound/ U.S. dollar market during regular European trading hours and 0 otherwise.

---

[13] Bollerslev-Ghysel benchmark dataset

Summary measures

- Consider the daily percentage nominal returns and the dummy variable:

```
> ret <- dmbp$V1
> days <- dmbp$V2
```

- The dummy variable should be stored as a factor. We add a vector of labels for the levels (0 ="Not Monday" and 1 ="Monday").

```
> days <- factor(dmbp$V2, labels = c("Not Monday", "Monday"))
```

Summary measures

In order to obtain the absolute frequencies of a qualitative or quantitative discrete variable, we use the function `table`.

```
> table(days)

days
Not Monday    Monday
      1518       456
```

Summary measures

- R offers functions to compute summary measures for quantitative variables.
- These functions operate on a vector x.

R function	Description
mean(x)	arithmetic mean of x
median(x)	median of x
var(x)	variance of x
sd(x)	standard deviation of x
quantile(x)	quantiles of x
range(x)	minimum and maximum values of x
IQR(x)	intequartile range of x
diff(x)	lagged differences of x

Summary measures

- In order to compute the mean or arithmetic average we use the function `mean`.

  ```
  > mean(ret)
  [1] -0.01643
  ```

- Note that this is equivalent to:

  ```
  > sum(ret)/length(ret)
  [1] -0.01643
  ```

- The median is computed in R with the function `median`.

  ```
  > median(ret)
  [1] -0.0006917
  ```

Summary measures

We calculate quantiles in R with the function `quantile`.

```
> quantile(ret)

          0%          25%          50%          75%         100%
-2.1442953   -0.2250333   -0.0006917    0.2228638    3.1725953
```

By default we obtain the minimum, the maximum, and the three quartiles. It is also possible to obtain other quantiles. For example, if we want the deciles:

```
> pdec <- seq(0, 1, by = 0.1)
> pdec

 [1] 0.0 0.1 0.2 0.3 0.4 0.5 0.6 0.7 0.8 0.9 1.0

> quantile(ret, pdec)

          0%          10%          20%          30%          40%
-2.1442953   -0.5452250   -0.3039233   -0.1602042   -0.0741588
         50%          60%          70%          80%          90%
-0.0006917    0.0738793    0.1686301    0.2866182    0.4927465
        100%
  3.1725953
```

Summary measures

The interquartile range (IQR) is the distance between the 75th percentile and the 25th percentile. It can be computed with the function IQR or using the quantile function.

```
> IQR(ret)
[1] 0.4479
> quantile(ret, 0.75) - quantile(ret, 0.25) # Equivalent to IQR
  75%
0.4479
```

Summary measures

The function `var` computes the variance of a vector of length n according to the formula:

$$\frac{1}{n-1} \sum_{i=1}^{n} (x_i - \bar{x})^2$$

```
> var(ret) # Variance
[1] 0.2211
>sd(ret) # Standard deviation
[1] 0.4702
>sqrt(var(ret)) # Equivalent to sd
[1] 0.4702
```

The apply family of functions

- There is an important family of functions in R that apply a function to subsets of some data structure.

- These functions are `apply` (for matrices and arrays), `lapply` and `sapply` (for lists), `mapply` (multivariate verion of `sapply`) and `tapply` (for summarizing data sets divided into groups by some factor).

The apply family of functions

- The function apply can be used to apply a function to the rows (second argument equal to 1) or columns (second argument equal to 2) of a matrix. [14]

```
> a
     [,1] [,2] [,3]
[1,]   10   12   14
[2,]   11   13   15

> apply(a, 1, sum)   # Apply sum to rows

[1] 36 39

> apply(a, 2, mean)   # Apply mean to columns

[1] 10.5 12.5 14.5
```

- The result is equivalent to:

```
> rowSums(a) # form row sums

[1] 36 39

> colMeans(a) # form column means

[1] 10.5 12.5 14.5
```

The apply family of functions

  Recall that the variable days takes the value of 1 on Mondays and other days following no trading in the Deutschemark or British pound/ U.S. dollar market during regular European and 0 otherwise.

  If we want to compute the mean daily percentage nominal returns grouped by days (0 or 1), we can use the tapply function.

```
> tapply(ret, days, mean) # mean daily % return grouped by days

Not Monday      Monday
  -0.01256    -0.02930
```

  Note that we could also use logical conditions:

```
> mean(ret[days == "Not Monday"]) # Mean of returns for not Monday
[1] -0.01256
>mean(ret[days == "Monday"]) # Mean of returns for Monday
[1] -0.0293
```

The apply family of functions

We can pass additional arguments to `tapply` . For instance, if we want the quantiles 0.2 and 0.4 of the daily percentage nominal returns grouped by `days`, we can write:

```
> tapply(ret, days, quantile, c(0.2, 0.4))
$ Not Monday
      20%      40%
-0.28296 -0.07245

$Monday
      20%      40%
-0.35190 -0.08952
```

The apply family of functions

We can also summarize by group:

```
> tapply(ret, days, summary) # summarize return grouped by days
$ Not Monday
    Min. 1st Qu.  Median   Mean 3rd Qu.    Max.
-1.9100 -0.2120  0.0009 -0.0126  0.2210  2.2000

$Monday
    Min. 1st Qu.  Median   Mean 3rd Qu.    Max.
 -2.140  -0.259  -0.007  -0.029   0.244   3.170
```

Table of contents. Plotting with R

Plots in R

- R includes tools to display a wide variety of statistical graphs.
- There are general packages for basic graphics programming (graphics, lattice) and many other R packages that provide specialized graphics (rgl, ggplot2, ...). For some examples type:

```
> demo(graphics)
```

- There are two main groups of plotting commands:
  - High-level plotting functions: create a new plot on the graphics device.
  - Low-level plotting functions: add more information to an existing plot.

 W. N. Venables, D. M. Smith and the R Core Team (2012).
An Introduction to R. Notes on R: A Programming Environment for Data Analysis and
Graphics. ISBN 3-900051-12-7. (Chapter 12)
http://cran.r-project.org/doc/manuals/R-intro.pdf

 W. Chang (2012).
R Graphics Cookbook. O'Reilly Media, Inc. ISBN 1449363105 Google books

The plot function

- The basic plotting function in R is plot.
- The function plot is a generic function (it can be applied to different types of objects).

```
> methods(plot)
 1   plot.acf*           plot.data.frame*
[3]  plot.decomposed.ts* plot.default
[5]  plot.dendrogram*    plot.density
[7]  plot.ecdf           plot.factor*
[9]  plot.formula*       plot.function
....
```

The plot function

A scatterplot of y against x is available using the `plot` function.

```
> x <- seq(-10, 10, length = 100)
> y <- x^2
> plot(x, y)
```

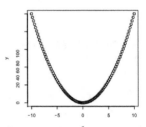

This is equivalent to supplying only the first argument as either a list containing two elements x and y or a two-column matrix.

```
> plot(list(x = x, y = y))
> plot(cbind(x, y))
```

Variables to be plotted can also be given in a formula notation. A formula is an expression of a relationship between the dependent variables (on the left), and the independent variables (on the right), with a tilde ~ as a separator.

```
> plot(y ~ x) # The formula means that y is explained by x
```

The plot function

Note that the following code plots the values in the vector y against their index.

```
> # One vector argument
> plot(y)
```

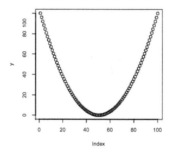

The plot function

If the argument is a factor, the `plot` function produces a bar-plot.

```
> # One factor argument
> blood <- c("AB", "A", "A", "B",
+       "A", "0", "B", "B", "AB")
> fblood <- factor(blood)
> plot(fblood)
```

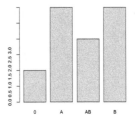

If the argument is a time series, the `plot` function produces a time-series plot.

```
> # Time series argument
> plot(AirPassengers)
```

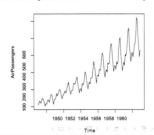

Arguments for the plot function

Here we list some of the arguments of the plot function. Check the help file for plot.default.

Argument	Description
type	Type of plot. Use type = p for points (default), type = 1 for lines, type = h for vertical lines, type = s for stairs steps, ...
main	Title on the graphic
sub	Subtitle on the graphic
xlabel	Labels for the x-axis
ylabel	Labels for the y-axis
ann	Logical value indicating whether the default annotation (title and axis labels) should appear
xlim	Specify the x-axis limits, for example xlim = c(0, 10)
ylim	Specify the y-axis limits
asp	Aspect ratio y/x. Set asp = 1 for same scale distance
axes	Logical value indicating whether both axes should be drawn

The plot function (and other graphing functions) take extra graphical parameters that can control different aspects of the graphic. Check the help file for par.

Argument	Description
col	The colors for lines and points
lty	When lines are plotted, specifies the type of line to be drawn
lwd	The thickness of lines
pch	The style of point

Arguments for the plot function

Here we show some examples [16].

```
> plot(x, y, type = "l", lty = 2, col = "red", lwd = 2, xlab = "x",
+       ylab = "y", main = "Plot function")
> plot(fblood, main = "Bar plot", col = "green", ylab = "Absolute freq")
> plot(AirPassengers, main = "Time Series", col = 4, lwd = 3)
```

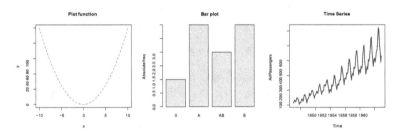

Adding extra information to an existing plot

- Low-level plotting functions can be used to add extra information (points, lines, text, a legend,...) to an existing plot.

- Low-level plotting functions can be executed once a high-level plot has been created. Some of the basic low-level plot functions to add components to the plot region are:

R function	Description
lines	adds a line to a plot
points	adds points to a plot
abline	adds a straight line to a plot
text	adds text to plot
legend	adds a legend to a plot

Adding extra information to an existing plot

For instance if we want to represent the sine function and then add the cosine function to the plot, we write: [17]

```
> x <- seq(0, 2 * pi, length = 100)
> y1 <- sin(x)
> plot(x, y1, type = "l", col = 2,
+      lty = 2, ylab = "y")
> y2 <- cos(x)
> lines(x, y2, col = 3, lwd = 2)
```

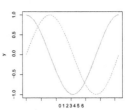

Now, we add a solid point in blue at $(2, 3)$, some text [14], a vertical line at $\frac{5\pi}{4}$ and a legend to the plot. [18]

```
> points(pi, 0, col = 4, pch = 19)
> text(pi, 0, "Point", pos = 3)
> abline(v = 5 * pi/4, col = 4)
> legend("bottomleft", c("Sine",
+      "Cosine"), col = c(2,
+      3), lty = c(2, 1))
```

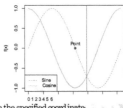

---

[14] The argument pos = 3 of the text function places the text above the specified coordinate.

Adding extra information to an existing plot

We can also annotate graphs outside the plot region. Here we list some of the functions to do this:

R function	Description
title	add labels to a plot
mtext	add text to the margins
axis	add an axis to the plot

Adding extra information to an existing plot

```
> x <- seq(0, 2 * pi, length = 100)
> y1 <- sin(x)
> plot(x, y1, type = "l", col = 2, lty = 2, ann = FALSE, axes = FALSE)
> axis(side = 1) # axis below
> axis(side = 4) # axis on the right
> title(main = "Title of the plot", xlab = "x label")
> mtext("This text is written in the left, line 0", side = 2, line = 0)
> mtext("This text is written in the left, line 1", side = 2, line = 1)
```

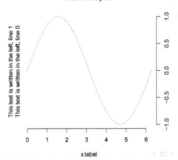

Multiple graphs in one panel

We can combine multiple plots into one overall graph, using the function `par` and the argument `mfrow`. The argument `mfrow=c(nrows, ncols)` creates a matrix of nrows ✗ncols plots that are filled in by row. For example:

```
> x <- seq(0, 2 * pi, length = 100)
> y1 <- sin(x)
> y2 <- cos(x)
> par(mfrow = c(1, 2)) # Layout with one row and two columns
> plot(x, y1, type = "l", main = "Sine function")
> plot(x, y2, type = "l", main = "Cosine function")
```

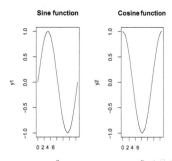

Other high-level plots

Apart from the `plot` function, there are other high-level plotting functions in R. Here we list some of them:

R function	Description
barplot	create a bar plot with vertical or horizontal bars
pie	draw a pie chart
hist	computes a histogram of the given data values
boxplot	produce box-and-whisker plot
persp	plot for three-dimensional data

As with the `plot` function, graphical parameters and low-level plotting functions can be used to add extra information.

Other high-level plots

For example, for the `dmbp` data set in package `rugarch`, we draw a barplot for the dummy variable:

```
> data(dmbp)
> ret <- dmbp$V1
> days <- factor(dmbp$V2,
+       labels = c("Not Monday",
+           "Monday"))
> freq <- table(days)
> barplot(freq, main = "Bar plot",
+     col = c(2, 3))
```

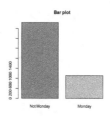

Now, we represent the same information with a pie chart:

```
> pie(freq, main = "Pie chart",
+     col = c(2, 3))
```

Other high-level plots

- We represent the histogram[15] for ret and the kernel density estimate:[16]

```
> hist(ret, freq = FALSE, col = 4,
+     ylim = c(0, 1))
> lines(density(ret, bw = 0.25),
+     col = 2, lwd = 2)
```

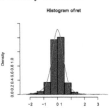

- Now, we represent the boxplot of ret:

```
> boxplot(ret) # Boxplot for ret
> boxplot(ret ~ days) # Boxplot for ret according to days
```

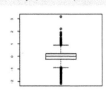
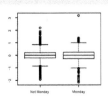

---

[15] The argument freq = FALSE plots a relative frequency density histogram (total area of one)
[16] The argument bw is the smoothing bandwidth to be used

Other high-level plots

- As example of three-dimensional plot, let us represent with the persp function the density of the standard bivariate normal distribution.

- The dnorm2d function in the fMultivar package computes the density for the bivariate normal distribution function at a given point (x, y). For example:

```
> library(fMultivar)
> dnorm2d(x = 0, y = 0, rho = 0) # rho is the correlation parameter

[1] 0.1592
attr(, "control")
rho
  0
```

Other high-level plots

The persp function requires vectors x and y containing the coordinates of the grid over which the function we want to represent is evaluated. The outer function evaluates a given function for each pair for each pair (x[i], y[j]).

```
> x <- seq(-3, 3, length = 50)
> y <- seq(-3, 3, length = 50)
> z <- outer(x, y, dnorm2d)
> persp(x, y, z, col = "lightblue",
+       theta = 135, phi = 30)
```

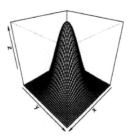

Probability distributions in R

R has four primary functions to work with distributions. Each function has a one letter prefix followed by the root name of the distribution we want to work with.

R prefix	Description
d	probability mass function (discrete distributions) or density function (continuous distributions)
p	cumulative probability or distribution function
q	quantiles of the distribution
r	random generation from the distribution

Here we list some of the probability distributions supported by R.

Distribution	R sufix		Distribution	R sufix
Binomial	binom		Uniform	unif
Geometric	geom		Normal	norm
Poisson	pois		Exponential	exp
Negative binomial	nbinom		Gamma	gamma

For example, the function dnorm is used to compute the probability density function of the normal distribution. The function pbinom is used to compute the distribution function of the binomial distribution. The function qpois is used to compute quantiles of the Poisson distribution. The function runif is used to generate random numbers from the continuous uniform distribution.

Probability distributions in R

We can represent the probability mass function and the cumulative distribution function of a binomial distribution. For example, for a Bin(20 0 3):

```r
> n <- 20
> p <- 0.3
> k <- 0:n # The Binomial distribution takes values 0,...,n
> plot(k, dbinom(k, n, p), type = "h", main = "Binomial mass")
> plot(k, pbinom(k, n, p), type = "s", main = "Binomial distribution")
```

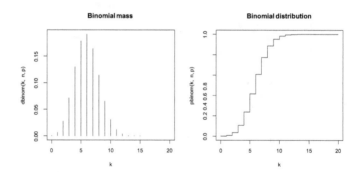

Probability distributions in R

We can represent the density function and the cumulative distribution function of a Normal distribution. For example, for a standard normal N(0,1):

```
> x <- seq(-4, 4, length = 100)
> plot(x, dnorm(x), type = "l", main = "Normal density")
> plot(x, pnorm(x), type = "l", main = "Normal distribution")
```

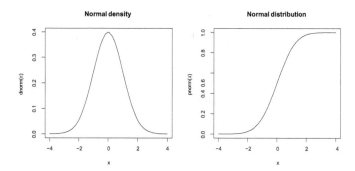

Probability distributions in R

We can represent the density functions of different normal random variables:

```
> x <- seq(-6, 6, length = 100)
> plot(x, dnorm(x), type = "l", main = "Normal density")
> lines(x, dnorm(x, mean = 1), col = 2) # Red: mean = 1, sd = 1
> lines(x, dnorm(x, sd = 1.5), col = 3) # Green: mean = 0, sd = 1.5
> lines(x, dnorm(x, -1, 2), col = 4) # Blue: mean = -1, sd = 2
```

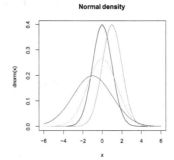

Probability distributions in R

- Here we represent the histogram of 1000 random numbers generated from a standard normal distribution. In blue, we add the kernel density estimate and, in red, we represent the density function of the standard normal:

```
> xgen <- rnorm(1000) # Random numbers from a standard normal
> hist(xgen, freq = FALSE) # Histogram of the generated sample
> lines(density(xgen), col = 4) # In blue, kernel density estimate
> curve(dnorm, -4, 4, col = 2, add = TRUE) # In red, normal density
```

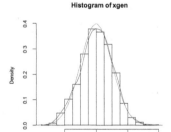

Histogram of xgen

Time series plots

- R also includes tools for plotting time series data.
- The plot function has a method for the class ts.

```
> data(AirPassengers) # ts class
> plot(AirPassengers) # Method plot.ts
```

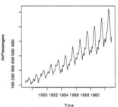

- The plot function has a method for the class timeSeries defined in the library timeSeries (plot.timeSeries).

```
> library(timeSeries)
> data(MSFT) # timeSeries class
> plot(MSFT) # Method plot.timeSeries
```

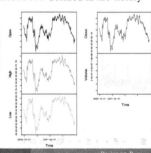

Time series plots

For multivariate time series, we can decide to plot the series separately with a common time axis (plot.type="multiple") or on a single plot (plot.type="single").

```
> plot(MSFT[, c("High", "Low")], plot.type = "multiple")
> plot(MSFT[, c("High", "Low")], plot.type = "single")
```

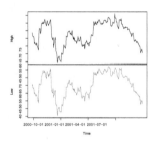 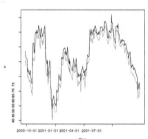

Time series plots

See what happens if we represent the high prices and the volume on the same plot. It would be more appropriate to use two different scales on the same plot.

```
> plot(MSFT[, c("High", "Volume")], plot.type = "multiple")
> plot(MSFT[, c("High", "Volume")], plot.type = "single")
```

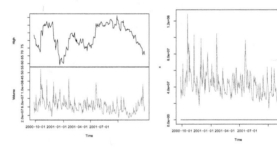

Time series plots

- We can define two different scales on the same plot. For that, we create a first plot and set par(new = TRUE) to prevent R from clearing the graphics device. Then we create the second plot with axes = FALSE and ann = FALSE. Finally we add a new axis and an axis label on the right-hand side.

```
> plot(MSFT[, "High"])
> par(new = TRUE) # Not clean the frame before drawing
> plot(MSFT[, "Volume"], axes = FALSE, ann = FALSE, col = 2)
> axis(4) # New axis on the right-hand side
> mtext("Volume", 4)
```

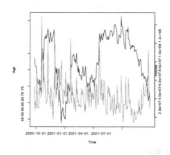

Exporting graphics

By default, graphical operations send the outcome to a graphical window. However, we can also export the graphic into an external file

1. Start the graphics device driver for producing the file. You can use pdf, jpeg, postscript,... (see the help file for Devices).
2. Write the plotting commands to make graphs. R sends all graphs to the file, and the graphic output will not appear on the screen.
3. Close the file by typing dev.off().

```
> jpeg("myplot1.jpeg")
> plot(MSFT[, c("High", "Low")], main = "Time Series")
> mtext("MSFT data set", 4)
> dev.off() # shuts down the current device
```

```
> pdf("myplot2.pdf")
> plot(MSFT[, c("High", "Low")], main = "Time Series")
> mtext("MSFT data set", 4)
> dev.off() # shuts down the current device
```

Exporting graphics

R can also generate high-quality vector (PDF, PostScript and SVG) and bitmap (PNG, JPEG, TIFF) files with the package Cairo.

```
> library(Cairo)
> CairoSVG("myplot3.svg")
> plot(MSFT[, c("High", "Low")], main = "Time Series")
> mtext("MSFT data set", 4)
> dev.off()
```

```
> CairoPDF("myplot4.pdf")
> plot(MSFT[, c("High", "Low")], main = "Time Series")
> mtext("MSFT data set", 4)
> dev.off()
```

Table of contents. Programming with R

Control structures

- R statements mainly consist of expressions to be evaluated.
- Control flow refers to the order in which the instructions or function calls of a program are executed or evaluated.
- There are different kinds of control flow statements:
  - executing a set of statements only if some condition is met.
  - executing a set of statements a given number of times.
  - executing a set of statements until some condition is met.
  - stop executing one thing or quit entirely.
  - ...
- R provides special syntax to use in common program structures.

 W. N. Venables, D. M. Smith and the R Core Team (2012).   ▶ More bibliography
An Introduction to R. Notes on R: A Programming Environment for Data Analysis and
Graphics. ISBN 3-900051-12-7. (Chapter 9)

http://cran.r-project.org/doc/manuals/R-intro.pdf

Conditional execution: if statements

- If statements allow us to do different things based on the value of some condition.
- Conditional expressions in R have this syntax:

```
if (condition) {
expressions 1 if true
}
else {
expressions 2 to do otherwise
}
```

where expressions 1 are evaluated if condition is TRUE and expressions 2 otherwise.

```
> x <- c(2, 1, 3)
> if(sqrt(9) > 2) {mean(x)} else {sum(x)}

[1] 2

> if(sqrt(9) > 4) {mean(x)} else {sum(x)}

[1] 6
```

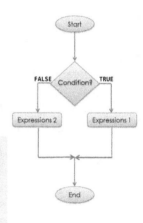

- The else part is optional.

Conditional execution: if statements

There is also a vectorized version of the if statements with the function ifelse.

```
> x <- c(2, 1, 3, 6, 8, 1)
> y <- ifelse(x > 3, mean(x), sum(x))
> y

[1] 21.0 21.0 21.0 3.5 3.5 21.0
```

Repetitive execution: for loops, repeat and while

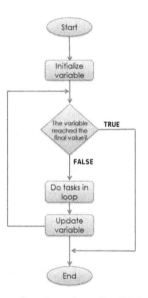

- In computer programming, when we want to repeatedly carry out some computation we use loops.
- A for loop will repeat a given code a certain number of times. In R a for loop has this syntax:

    ```
    for (variable in vector) {
    commands
    }
    ```

- The loop sets the value of variable equal to each element of the vector and each time evaluates the given commands.

```
> for (i in 1:5) {print(i)}

[1] 1
[1] 2
[1] 3
[1] 4
[1] 5
```

Repetitive execution: for loops, repeat and while

Note that the variable that is set in a for loop is changed in the calling environment.

```
> i <- 1
> for (i in seq(5, 10, 2)) {print(i)}

[1] 5
[1] 7
[1] 9

> i

[1] 9
```

Repetitive execution: for loops, repeat and while

Remember that you can often avoid looping by using vectorized operations. For example, suppose that we want to form row sums for a matrix.

```
> a <- matrix(10:15, 2, 3)
> a

     [,1] [,2] [,3]
[1,]   10   12   14
[2,]   11   13   15

> nr<-nrow(a) # number of rows is a
> sumr<-numeric(nr) # initialize a vector of length nr
> for(i in 1:nr) {sumr[i] <- sum(a[i, ])}
> sumr

[1] 36 39
```

This is equivalent to:

```
> rowSums(a)

[1] 36 39
>apply(a, 1, sum)

[1] 36 39
```

Repetitive execution: for loops, repeat and while

- Another looping structure is repeat, which repeats the same expression. The syntax is:

```
repeat{
expression
}
```

- To stop repeating the expression, use the keyword break. (19)

```
> x <- 7
> repeat{print(x); x <- x + 2; if(x > 10) {break}}

[1] 7
[1] 9
```

- Note that the statement must include a test that determines when to break the execution of the loop.

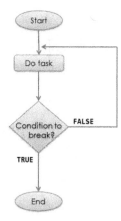

Repetitive execution: for loops, repeat and while

The while structure evaluates a expression as long as a stated condition is TRUE. The syntax is:

```
while(condition) {
    expression
}
```

For example.

```
> x <- 0
> while(x < 10) {print(x); x <- x + 5}

[1] 0
[1] 5
```

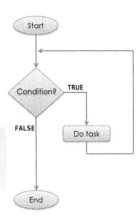

Writing functions

- In R there are many built-in functions: plot, summary, sum, ...
- There are also thousands of functions contributed by the R community (check the help file of any library).
- You can also write your own function for a particular problem.

 W. N. Venables, D. M. Smith and the R Core Team (2012). More bibliography
An Introduction to R. Notes on R: A Programming Environment for Data Analysis and
Graphics. ISBN 3-900051-12-7. (Chapter 10)
http://cran.r-project.org/doc/manuals/R-intro.pdf

Writing functions

- Let us first examine one of the functions provided in the base R code, the mad function, that computes the median of the absolute deviations from the median.

```
> mad
function (x, center = median(x), constant = 1.4826, na.rm = FALSE,
    low = FALSE, high = FALSE)
{
    if (na.rm)
        x <- x[!is.na(x)]
    n <- length(x)
    constant * if ((low || high) && n%%2 == 0) {
        if (low && high)
            stop("'low' and 'high' cannot be both TRUE")
        n2 <- n%/%2 + as.integer(high)
        sort(abs(x - center), partial = n2)[n2]
    }
    else median(abs(x - center))
}
....
```

Writing functions

- The syntax for writing a function is:

  ```
  function.name <- function(arguments) {
  body of the function
  return(return value)
  }
  ```

- Create a new script and write the following code.

  ```
  # My first R function.
  # Given a number x, this function returns 2x+5.
  myf1 <- function(x) {
      y <- 2 * x + 5
      return(y)
  }
  ```

- Compile the function and write:

  ```
  > myf1(2)
  [1] 9
  >myf1(5)
  [1] 15
  ```

Writing functions

- The return statement can be omitted since by default R will return the last evaluated expression.

```
myf2 <- function(x) {
    2 * x + 5
}
```

- Compile the function and write:

```
> myf2(2)
[1] 9
>myf2(5)
[1] 15
```

Writing functions

- Arguments can be given default values

```
myf3 <- function(x = 3) {
    2 * x + 5
}
```

- Compile the function and write:

```
> myf3() # x takes the default value
[1] 11
> myf3(5) # overrides the default value
[1] 15
```

Writing functions

Functions can have several arguments.

```
myf4 <- function(x = 3, y = 5) {
    2 * x + y + 5
}
```

Compile the function and write:

```
> myf4() # default values
[1] 16
>myf4(4) # x = 4, y = default
[1] 18
>myf4(4, 6) # x = 4, y = 6 [positional matching]
[1] 19
>myf4(y = 4, x = 3) # x = 3, y = 4 [matching by name]
[1] 15
```

Writing functions

An R function can call other R functions.

```
myf5 <- function(x, powx) {
    plot(x, x^powx, main = paste("x to the power of ", powx))
}
```

Compile the function and write:

```
> x <- seq(-10, 10, length = 100)
> myf5(x, 2)   # Plot y=x^2
> myf5(x, 3)   # Plot y=x^3
```

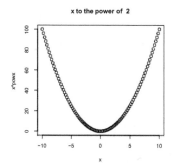
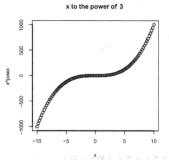

Writing functions

Suppose we want to allow the user to change the look of the plot. We can pass extra arguments to another function or write a function that accepts a variable number of arguments. To do this in R, specify an ellipsis (. . .) in the arguments to the function.

```
myf6 <- function(x, powx, ...) {
  plot(x, x^powx, main = paste("x to the power of ", powx), ...)
}
```

Writing functions

- Compile the function and write:

```
> x <- seq(-10, 10, length = 100)
> myf6(x, 2, col = 2, ylab = "Function") # Plot y=x^2
> myf6(x, 3, type = "l", col = 3) # Plot y=x^3
```

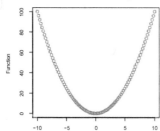

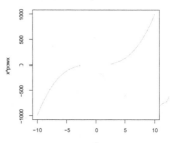

Writing functions

An R function is allowed to return only a single R object. Lists are useful in R to return multiple values.

```
myf5 <- function(x = 3, y = 5) {
    z <- 2 * x + y + 5
    return(list(input = c(x, y), result = z))
}
```

Compile the function and write:

```
> out <- myf5(4, 6)
> class(out)
[1] "list"
> names(out)
[1] "input" "result"
>out$input
[1] 4 6
>out$result
[1] 19
```

Writing functions

Functions can include loops and conditional statements.

```
myf6 <- function(x = 3, y = 5) {
    if (x > 2) {
        print("x is greater than 2")
        return(3 * y + 2)
    } else {
        print("x is lower than or equal to 2")
        return(3 * y + 5)
    }
}
```

Compile the function and write:

```
> myf6(5, 3)
[1] "x is greater than 2"
[1] 11

> myf6(1, 3)
[1] "x is lower than or equal to 2"
[1] 14
```

Execution time

- Functions can include loops and conditional statements.

```
myrowSums <- function(a) {
    nr <- nrow(a) # number of rows is a
    sumr <- numeric(nr) # initialize a vector of length nr
    for (i in 1:nr) {
        sumr[i] <- sum(a[i, ])
    }
    return(sumr)
}
```

- Compile the function and write:

```
> a <- matrix(10:15, 2, 3)
> myrowSums(a)

[1] 36 39
```

- This is equivalent to:

```
> rowSums(a)

[1] 36 39
>apply(a, 1, sum)

[1] 36 39
```

Execution time

- The function system.time measures the execution time. [20]
- Let us compare the performance of the functions myrowSums, rowSums and apply, on a matrix of 2 ×10 numbers from a standard normal distribution.

```
> a <- matrix(rnorm(2 * 10^6), nc = 2)
> system.time(myrowSums(a))
    user system elapsed
    2.76    0.00    2.76

>system.time(rowSums(a))
user system elapsed
       0       0       0
> system.time(apply(a, 1, sum))
  user system elapsed
  4.63    0.01    4.65
```

Table of contents. RStudio

Dynamic reports using LATEX

- R includes a powerful and flexible system (Sweave) for creating dynamic reports using LATEX. Sweave enables the embedding of R code within LATEX documents to generate a PDF file that includes narrative and analysis, graphics, code, and the results of computations.

- knitr is an R package that adds many new capabilities to Sweave and is also fully supported by RStudio.

- To use Sweave or knitr to create PDF reports, you will need to have LATEXinstalled on your system.

- Select Sweave or knitr from the menu Tools ɪ Options, in the Sweave dialog.

From http://www.rstudio.com/ide/docs/authoring/overview

Sweave

- To start a new Sweave document, select "Weave Rnw files using Sweave" in the menu Tools ı   Options, in the Sweave dialog.

- Go to File ı   New and select "R Sweave".

- This opens a basic Sweave template where you can enter text and L^AT_EXcommands.

- R code to be processed must be included into special blocks named code chunks. A code chunk is demarked with:

    ```
    <<>>=
      R code
    @
    ```

- You can compile the Sweave document into a PDF using the Compile PDF button on the toolbar.

F. Leisch (2002).
Sweave: Dynamic generation of statistical reports using literate data analysis. In Wolfgang Härdle and Bernd Rönz, editors, Compstat 2002 - Proceedings in Computational Statistics, pages 575-580. Physica Verlag, Heidelberg

http://www.stat.uni-muenchen.de/~leisch/Sweave/

Sweave

Here we show a simple example of Sweave document.

Sweave

- Sweave supports many options for code chunks that control how code chunks and their output are transfered to the .tex file.

- We write chunk options in the form `tag=value` like this:
  `<<tag1 = value1, tag2 = value2, tag3 = value3>>`

- Some of the most common options are:
  - echo: logical (by default, TRUE). Include R code in the output file?
  - eval: logical (by default, TRUE). If FALSE, the code chunk is not evaluated, and hence no text or graphical output produced.
  - fig: logical (by default, FALSE). Indicating whether the code chunk produces graphical output.
  - width: numeric width of figures in inch.
  - height: numeric height of figures in inch.

- To print an R expression use a \Sexpr statement.

Sweave

Here we show a simple example of Sweave options for code chunks.

knitr

- The knitr package solves some long-standing problems in Sweave.
- To start a new knitr document, select "Weave Rnw files using knitr" in the menu Tools ı Options, in the Sweave dialog.
- Go to File ı New and select "R Sweave".
- This opens a basic knitr template where you can enter text and LATEX commands.
- R code to be processed must be included into special blocks named code chunks. A code chunk in knitr is also demarked with:

```
<<>>=
  R code
@
```

- You can compile the knitr document into a PDF using the Compile PDF button on the toolbar.

 Y. Xie (2013).
Dynamic Documents with R and knitr. Chapman and Hall/CRC. ISBN 978-1482203530
http://yihui.name/knitr/

Table of contents. Hints and tips in R

Hints and tips in R

1. You can change the default settings of the R GUI (font, size, console colors, ...) in the menu Edit ⅰ GUI preferences...

2. The standard R prompt > and other default settings can be modified. For example:

```
> options(prompt = "R> ", digits = 3, continue = "??")
```

replaces the standard R prompt > by R> and the standard prompt used for lines which continue + by ??. The option `digits = 3` reduces the number of digits shown when printing numbers.

1. R also includes automatic completions for function names and filenames. Type the Tab key to see a list of possible completions for a function or filenames.

2. Use the functions is.na, is.nan, is.finite and is.infinite to check whether an object is NA, NaN, Inf or -Inf, respectively.

```
> x <- sqrt(-4); y <- 1/0
> is.nan(x)

[1] TRUE

> is.finite(y)

[1] FALSE

> is.infinite(y)

[1] TRUE
```

Hints and tips in R

1. List of available CRAN Packages By Date of Publication. http://cran.r-project.org/web/packages/available_packages_by_date.html

2. You can obtain the list of data sets for a given package, for example the rugarch package:

```
> data(package = "rugarch")
```

7. Sweave enables the embedding of R code within LaTeX documents to generate a PDF file that includes text, graphics, code, and the results of computations. knitr is an R package that adds many new capabilities to Sweave. R Markdown is a format that enables easy authoring of reproducible web reports from R. Read more...

   - http://www.rstudio.com/ide/docs/authoring/overview,
   - http://www.rstudio.com/ide/docs/r_markdown.

Hints and tips in R

8. When using a function in R, the argument sequence may be given in an unnamed, positional form (positional matching). This means that you don't need to specify the argument name provided that you write it in the same position as in the argument list of the function. If a function has a large number of arguments and you don't know the order in which they are defined, you should specify the name of the argument you pass to the function (matching by name). It may be enough with the first part of the argument name (partial matching of names).

You can obtain the argument names and corresponding default values of a function with args. For example,

```
> args(read.table) # Argument list of read.table
```

1. A comma-separated values (CSV) file stores tabular data (numbers and text) in plain-text form. A CSV file consists of any number of records divided into fields separated by delimiters (typically comma or semicolon). In a tab-separated values (TSV) file, the data items are separated using tabs as a delimiter.

2. When exporting to CSV files, if the data contains the field delimiter (commas) then you must enclose text in quotes.

Hints and tips in R

11. TRUE and FALSE are reserved words denoting logical constants in the R language, whereas T and F are global variables whose initial values set to these. Logical vectors are coerced to integer vectors in contexts where a numerical value is required.

```
> x <- c(TRUE, FALSE, F, T, T)
> x

[1]  TRUE FALSE FALSE  TRUE  TRUE

> class(x)

[1] "logical"

> TRUE <- 5

Error: invalid (do_set) left-hand side to assignment
```

1. The subset function is another way to select variables and observations. See the help file for further information.

2. The double equal sign == is used for testing equality. This is to avoid confusion with the simple = symbol used for assignment.

Hints and tips in R

1. In general, the function `apply` applies a function to margins of an array. The second argument is the subscript which the function will be applied over.

```
> a <- array(data = 1:24, dim = c(3, 4, 2))
> a

, , 1

     [,1] [,2] [,3] [,4]
[1,]    1    4    7   10
[2,]    2    5    8   11
[3,]    3    6    9   12

, , 2

     [,1] [,2] [,3] [,4]
[1,]   13   16   19   22
[2,]   14   17   20   23
[3,]   15   18   21   24

> apply(a, 3, sum)

[1] 78 222
```

Hints and tips in R

15. Colors in R may be specified by index, name, hexadecimal, or RGB. For example, col = 1, col = "white", and col = "#FFFFFF" are equivalent. See a complete chart of R colors at http://research.stowers-institute.org/efg/R/Color/Chart/index.htm. You can also show all named colors with:

```
> demo(colors)
```

16. The function do.call allows the argument list of a function to be set up in advance of the call. For example,

```
> x <- seq(-10, 10, length = 100)
> y <- x^2
> plot(x, y, type = "l", lty = 2, col = "red", lwd = 2, xlab = "x",
+       ylab = "y", main = "Plot function")
```

is equivalent to

```
> plotargs <- list(x = x, y = y, type = "l", lty = 2, col = "red",
+       lwd = 2, xlab = "x", ylab = "y", main = "Plot function")
> do.call("plot", args = plotargs)
```

Hints and tips in R

17. You can also use the function curve to draw a curve corresponding to a function over a given interval.

```
> curve(sin, 0, 2 * pi, col = 2,
+     lty = 2, ylab = "y")
> curve(cos, 0, 2 * pi, add = TRUE,
+     col = 3, lwd = 2)
```

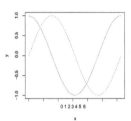

18. Mathematical expressions can be used for titles, subtitles, axis labels, etc. See the help file of plotmath. For some examples, type:

```
> demo(plotmath)
```

Hints and tips in R

1. There are two special reserved words in R to stop the execution in a loop:
   - next: it terminates evaluation of the body of the loop for the current iteration.
   - break: it terminates evaluation of the complete loop expression.

1. The function system.time returns the user time (CPU time charged for the execution of user instructions of the calling process), the system time (CPU time charged for execution by the system on behalf of the calling process) and the elapsed time (time we would have seen on a clock).

Table of contents. Bibliography

Books

J. Adler (2010).
R in a Nutshell. O'Reilly Media. ISBN 9781449383046.   Google books

W. J. Braun and D. J. Murdoch (2007).
A First Course in Statistical Programming with R. Cambridge University Press, Cambridge.
ISBN 978-0521872652. Google books

J. M. Chambers (2008).
Software for Data Analysis: Programming with R. Springer-Verlag New York. ISBN
9780387759364. Google books

W. Chang (2012).
R Graphics Cookbook. O'Reilly Media, Inc. ISBN 1449363105   Google books

M. J. Crawley (2012).
The R Book. Wiley. ISBN 9781118448960.   Google books

P. Dalgaard (2008).
Introductory Statistics with R. Springer. ISBN 9780387790534.   Google books

J. J. Faraway (2004).
Linear Models with R. Chapman Hall/CRC, Boca Raton, FL. ISBN 1-584-88425-8.
Google books

Books

C. Kleiber, and A. Zeileis (2008).
Applied econometrics with R. Springer Science+Business Media, LLC. ISBN 9780387773186.
Google books

J. Maindonald and J. Braun (2007).
Data Analysis and Graphics Using R. Cambridge University Press, Cambridge, 2nd edition.
ISBN 978-0-521-86116-8. Google books

L. Pace (2012).
Beginning R: An Introduction to Statistical Programming. Apress. ISBN 1430245557,
9781430245551. Google books

W. N. Venables, D. M. Smith and the R Core Team (2012).
An Introduction to R. Notes on R: A Programming Environment for Data Analysis and
Graphics. ISBN 3-900051-12-7.
http://cran.r-project.org/doc/manuals/R-intro.pdf

J. Verzani (2005).
Using R for Introductory Statistics. Chapman Hall/CRC, Boca Raton, FL. ISBN 1-584-
88450-9. Google books

A. F. Zuur, E. N. Ieno, and E. Meesters (2009).
A Beginner's Guide to R. Springer. ISBN 9780387938363. Google books

Lecture notes

useR! - International R User Conference.
This is the main meeting of the R user and developer community. You can download keynote lectures and presentation slides from:
http://www.r-project.org/conferences/

S. Højsgaard.
Department of Mathematical Sciences, Aalborg University, Denmark.
http://people.math.aau.dk/~sorenh/

P. Kuhnert and B. Venables.
CSIRO Mathematical and Information Sciences Cleveland, Australia.
http://www.csiro.au/en/Organisation-Structure/Divisions/
Mathematics-Informatics-and-Statistics/Rcoursenotes.aspx

R. Ripley.
Department of Statistics, University of Oxford
http://www.stats.ox.ac.uk/~ruth/

Online resources (blogs, tutorials, open books, search engines)

 R bloggers
http://www.r-bloggers.com/

 R User Groups
http://www.r-bloggers.com/RUG/

 Quick-R
http://www.statmethods.net/

 Resources to help you learn and use R.
IDRE Reseach Technology Group. University of California, Los Angeles.
http://www.ats.ucla.edu/stat/r/

 R Programming Wikibook
http://en.wikibooks.org/wiki/R_Programming

 R Seek
http://www.rseek.org/